Countries, Capitals and Flags of the World

North America

South America

Antarctica

Africa

Europe

Australia
and
Oceania

North America:
Area: 24,710,000 km^2 (9,540,000 sq mi) Population: 580 million Countries: 23

South America:
Area: 17,840,000 km^2 (6,890,000 sq mi) Population: 423 million Countries: 12

Europe:
Area: 10,180,000 km^2 (3,930,000 sq mi) Population: 747 million Countries: 50

Africa:
Area: 30,370,000 km^2 (11,730,000 sq mi) Population: 1.2 billion Countries: 54

Asia:
Area: 44,579,000 km^2 (17,212,000 sq mi) Population: 4.6 billion Countries: 48

Australia and Oceania:
Area: 8,525,989 km^2 (3,291,903 sq mi) Population: 41 million Countries: 14

Antarctica:
Area: 14,000,000 km^2 (5,400,000 sq mi) Population: 1,100 Countries: 0

Continent	Percent of all Earth ground	Continent	Percent of all Earth population
Asia	≈21.53%	Asia	≈60.04%
Africa	≈20.20%	Africa	≈15.35%
Europe	≈15.46%	Europe	≈10.50%
North America	≈14.92%	North America	≈7.80%
South America	≈11.89%	South America	≈5.70%
Australia and Oceania	≈5.70%	Australia and Oceania	≈0.53%
Total:	≈ 148.94 mln.km^2	Total:	≈ 7.6 Billion People

Surface	Area	Percent of Eart surface
Ground	148.95 mln. km^2	29.2%
Water	361.12 mln. km^2	70.8%
Total:	510.07 mln. km^2	

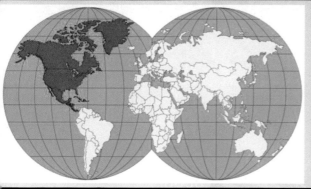

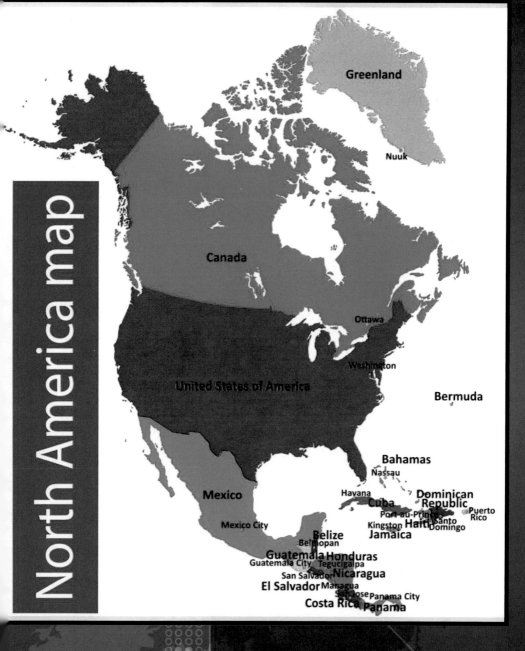

North America map

Greenland

Nuuk

Canada

Ottawa

Washington

Bermuda

United States of America

Mexico

Bahamas

Nassau

Havana

Mexico City

Cuba

Dominican
Republic

Puerto
Rico

Port-au-Prince

Santo
Domingo

Kingston

Haiti

Belize

Jamaica

Belmopan

Guatemala Honduras

Guatemala City   Tegucigalpa

San Salvador

Nicaragua

El Salvador

Managua

San Jose

Panama City

Costa Rica Panama

Country: Antigua and Barbuda **Capital:** Saint Johns **Area(km²):** 6,442 **Population:** 98,500	**Country:** Bahamas **Capital:** Nassau **Area(km²):** 13,940 **Population:** 395,900	**Country:** Barbados **Capital:** Bridgetown **Area(km²):** 430 **Population:** 287,600

Country: Belize **Capital:** Belmopan **Area(km²):** 22,966 **Population:** 402,100	**Country:** Canada **Capital:** Ottawa **Area(km²):** 9,976,139 **Population:** 38,067,900	**Country:** Costa Rica **Capital:** San Jose **Area(km²):** 51,100 **Population:** 5,126,500

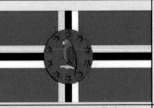

Country: Cuba **Capital:** Havana **Area(km²):** 110,860 **Population:** 11,317,500	**Country:** Dominica **Capital:** Roseau **Area(km²):** 754 **Population:** 72,100	**Country:** Dominican Republic **Capital:** Santo Domingo **Area(km²):** 48,730 **Population:** 10,953,700

Country: El Salvador **Capital:** San Salvador **Area(km²):** 21,040 **Population:** 6,509,000	**Country:** Grenada **Capital:** Saint Georges **Area(km²):** 340 **Population:** 113,000	**Country:** Guatemala **Capital:** Guatemala City **Area(km²):** 108,890 **Population:** 18,249,800

Country: Haiti
Capital: Port-au-Prince
Area(km²): 27,750
Population: 11,541,600

Country: Honduras
Capital: Tegucigalpa
Area(km²): 112,090
Population: 10,062,900

Country: Jamaica
Capital: Kingston
Area(km²): 10,990
Population: 2,973,400

Country: Mexico
Capital: Mexico City
Area(km²): 1,972,550
Population: 126,700,000

Country: Nicaragua
Capital: Managua
Area(km²): 129,494
Population: 6,702,300

Country: Panama
Capital: Panama City
Area(km²): 78,200
Population: 4,381,570

Country:
Saint Kitts and Nevis
Capital: Basseterre
Area(km²): 261
Population: 53,460

Country: Saint Lucia
Capital: Castries
Area(km²): 620
Population: 184,200

Country: Saint Vincent
and the Grenadines
Capital: Kingstown
Area(km²): 389
Population: 111,200

Country:
Trinidad and Tobago
Capital: Port-of-Spain
Area(km²): 5,128
Population: 1,403,400

Country:
United States of America
Capital: Washington
Area(km²): 9,522,057
Population: 331,900,000

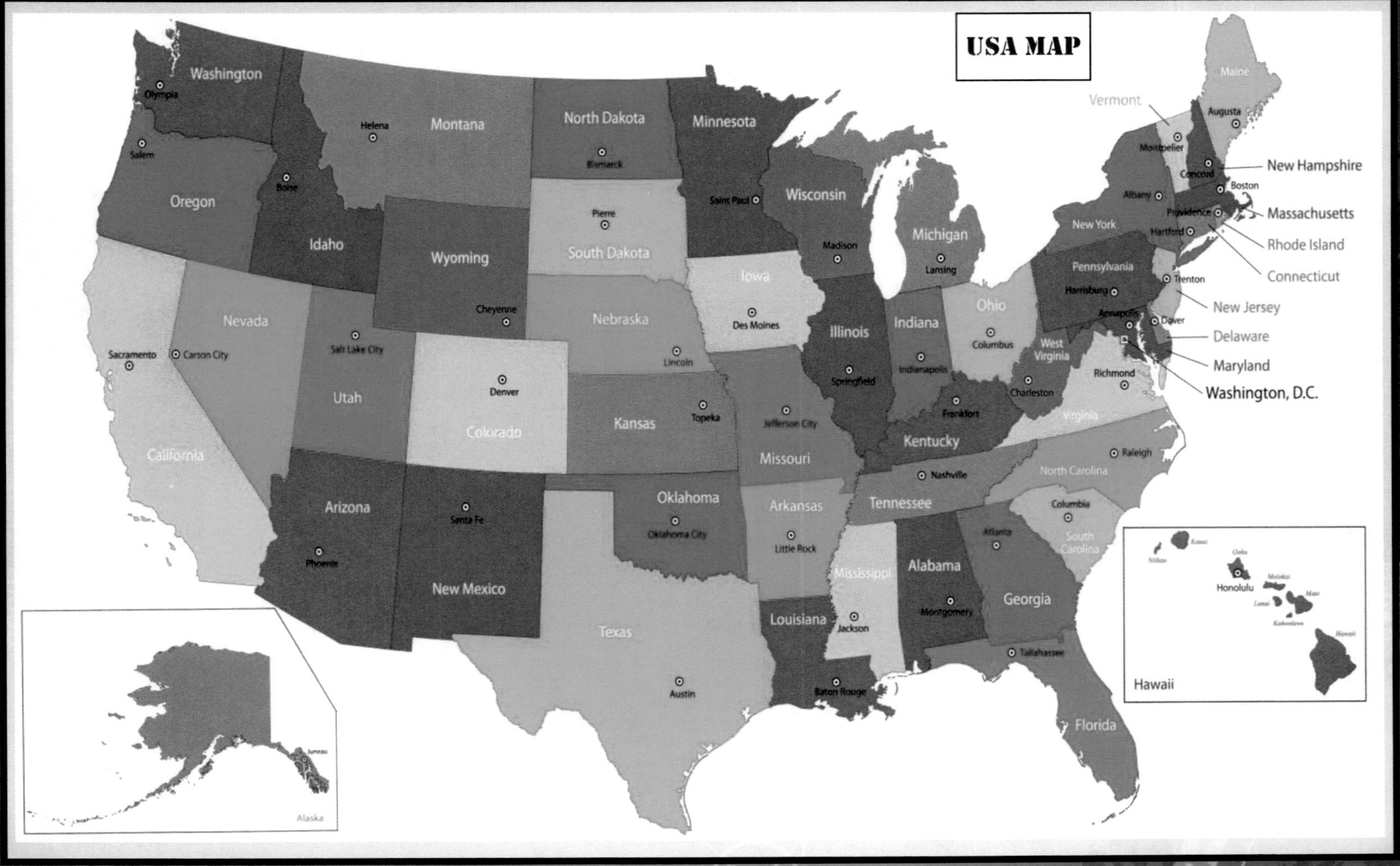
USA MAP
Washington
Olympia
Oregon
Salem
California
Sacramento
Nevada
Carson City
Idaho
Boise
Montana
Helena
Wyoming
Cheyenne
Utah
Salt Lake City
Arizona
Phoenix
Colorado
Denver
New Mexico
Santa Fe
North Dakota
Bismarck
South Dakota
Pierre
Nebraska
Lincoln
Kansas
Topeka
Oklahoma
Oklahoma City
Texas
Austin
Minnesota
Saint Paul
Iowa
Des Moines
Missouri
Jefferson City
Arkansas
Little Rock
Louisiana
Baton Rouge
Wisconsin
Madison
Illinois
Springfield
Mississippi
Jackson
Michigan
Lansing
Indiana
Indianapolis
Kentucky
Frankfort
Tennessee
Nashville
Alabama
Montgomery
Ohio
Columbus
West Virginia
Charleston
Georgia
Atlanta
Florida
Tallahassee
South Carolina
Columbia
North Carolina
Raleigh
Virginia
Richmond
Pennsylvania
Harrisburg
New York
Albany
Maine
Augusta
Vermont
Montpelier
New Hampshire
Concord
Massachusetts
Boston
Rhode Island
Providence
Connecticut
Hartford
New Jersey
Trenton
Delaware
Dover
Maryland
Annapolis
Washington, D.C.
Alaska
Juneau
Hawaii
Honolulu

CARIBBEAN MAP

Caribbean Map illustrating the Gulf of Mexico, Caribbean Sea, and surrounding countries and cities including:

- **United States cities:** Austin, San Antonio, Houston, New Orleans, Matamoros, Jacksonville, Tampa, Orlando, Miami
- **Mexico:** Puebla, Oaxaca, Merida, Cancun
- **Gulf of Mexico**
- **THE BAHAMAS** — Nassau
- **CUBA** — Havana
- **Cayman Is. (U.K.)**
- **JAMAICA** — Kingston
- **Navassa Island (U.K.)**
- **HAITI** — Port-au-Prince
- **DOMINICAN REPUBLIC** — Santiago, Santo Domingo
- **Turks and Caicos Island (U.K.)**
- **Puerto Rico (U.S.)** — San Juan
- **British Virgin Islands (U.K.)**
- **Anguilla (U.K.)**
- **ST. KITTS AND NEVIS**
- **ANTIGUA AND BARBUDA**
- **Montserrat (U.K.)**
- **Guadeloupe (FR.)**
- **DOMINICA**
- **Martinique (FR.)**
- **ST. LUCIA**
- **BARBADOS**
- **ST. VINCENT AND THE GRENADINES**
- **GRENADA**
- **Neth. Antilles (NETH.)**
- **Aruba (NETH.)**
- **TRINIDAD AND TOBAGO** — Pórt-of-Spain
- **Caribbean Sea**
- **GUATEMALA** — Guatemala
- **BELIZE** — Belmopan
- **EL SALVADOR** — San Salvador
- **HONDURAS** — Tegucigalpa
- **NICARAGUA** — Managua
- **COSTA RICA** — San Jose
- **PANAMA** — Panama, Colon
- **Isla del Coco**
- **VENEZUELA** — Caracas, Maracaibo, Valencia, Cuidad Guayana, Barranquilla, Cartagena, Cucuta, Medellin
- **Georgetown**

South America map

Caracas

Venezuela

Georgetown

Paramaribo

Cayenne

Bogota

Colombia

Guyana

Suriname

French Guiana

Quito

Ecuador

Peru

Brazil

Lima

La Paz

Bolivia

Brasilia

Paraguay

Chile

Asuncion

Argentina **Uruguay**

Santiago

Montevideo

Buenos Aires

Falkland Islands (UK)

Stanley

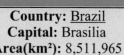

Country: Argentina
Capital: Buenos Aires
Area(km²): 2,766,890
Population: 45,605,800

Country: Bolivia
Capital: Sucre, La Paz
Area(km²): 1,098,580
Population: 11,783,700

Country: Brazil
Capital: Brasilia
Area(km²): 8,511,965
Population: 214,300,000

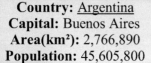
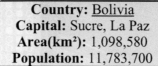
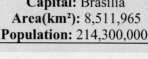

Country: Chile
Capital: Santiago
Area(km²): 756,950
Population: 19,212,200

Country: Colombia
Capital: Bogota
Area(km²): 1,138,910
Population: 51,265,800

Country: Ecuador
Capital: Quito
Area(km²): 283,560
Population: 17,888,400

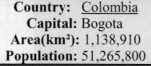

Country: Guyana
Capital: Georgetown
Area(km²): 214,970
Population: 790,300

Country: Paraguay
Capital: Asuncion
Area(km²): 406,750
Population: 7,219,600

Country: Peru
Capital: Lima
Area(km²): 1,285,220
Population: 33,359,400

Country: Suriname
Capital: Paramaribo
Area(km²): 163,270
Population: 590,290

Country: Uruguay
Capital: Montevideo
Area(km²): 176,220
Population: 3,482,100

Country: Venezuela
Capital: Caracas
Area(km²): 912,052
Population: 28,379,500

Not official

Historical

Country: French Guiana
(Overseas departments and
regions of France)
Capital: Cayenne
Area (km²): 83,534
Population: 294,070
Official flag - Flag of France

EUROPE

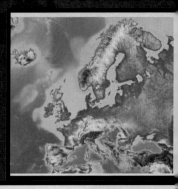

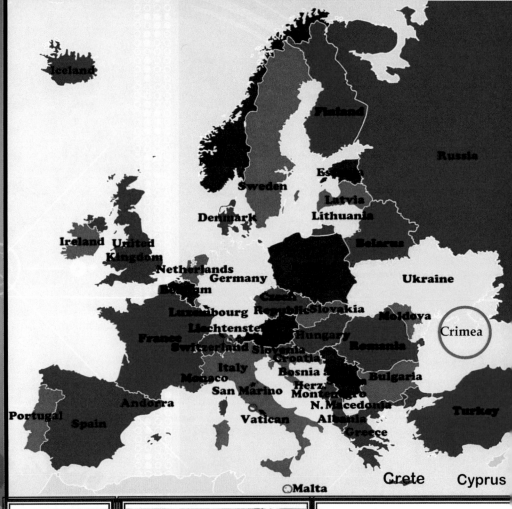

Iceland

Finland

Russia

Sweden

Estonia

Latvia

Denmark

Lithuania

Ireland United Kingdom

Belarus

Netherlands

Germany

Ukraine

Belgium

Czech Republic

Slovakia

Moldova

Luxembourg

Liechtenstein

Hungary

Crimea

France

Switzerland

Slovenia

Romania

Croatia

Italy

Bosnia and Herz.

Serbia

Bulgaria

Monaco

Montenegro

San Marino

Andorra

N. Macedonia

Turkey

Portugal

Spain

Vatican

Albania

Greece

Crete

Cyprus

○Malta

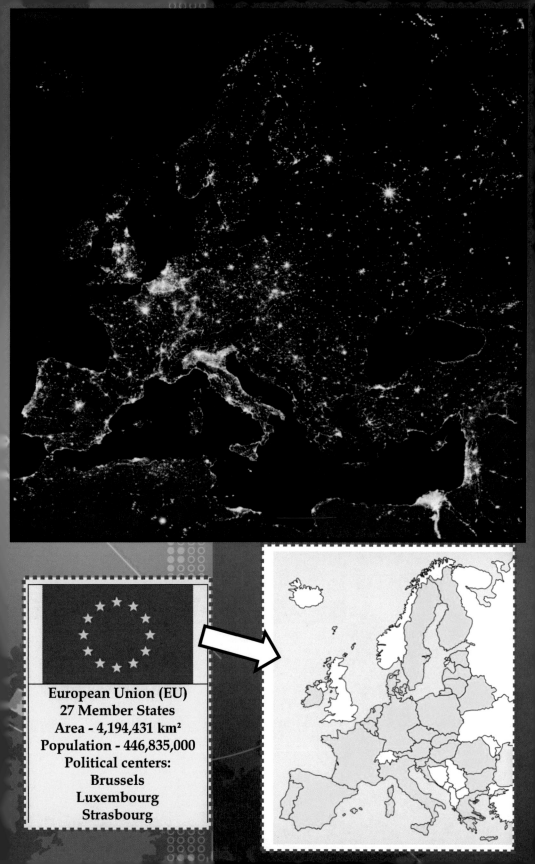

European Union (EU)
27 Member States
Area - 4,194,431 km²
Population - 446,835,000
Political centers:
Brussels
Luxembourg
Strasbourg

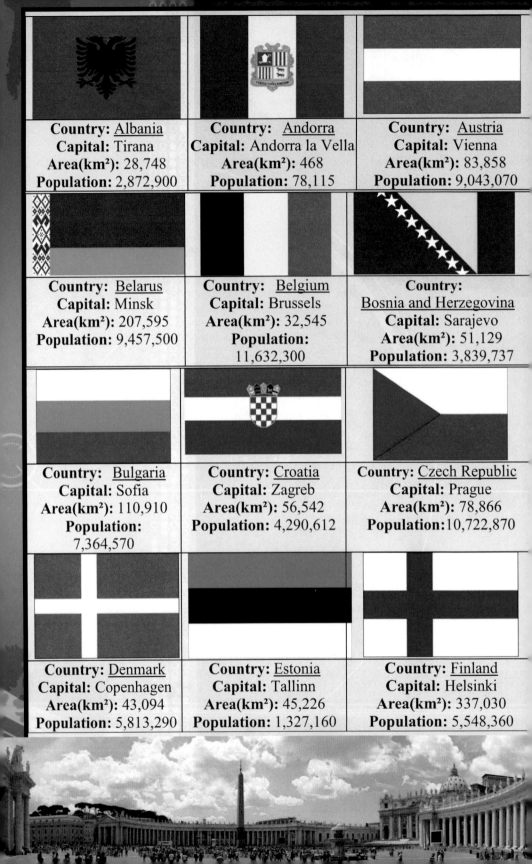

Country: <u>Albania</u>
Capital: Tirana
Area(km²): 28,748
Population: 2,872,900

Country: <u>Andorra</u>
Capital: Andorra la Vella
Area(km²): 468
Population: 78,115

Country: <u>Austria</u>
Capital: Vienna
Area(km²): 83,858
Population: 9,043,070

Country: <u>Belarus</u>
Capital: Minsk
Area(km²): 207,595
Population: 9,457,500

Country: <u>Belgium</u>
Capital: Brussels
Area(km²): 32,545
Population: 11,632,300

Country:
<u>Bosnia and Herzegovina</u>
Capital: Sarajevo
Area(km²): 51,129
Population: 3,839,737

Country: <u>Bulgaria</u>
Capital: Sofia
Area(km²): 110,910
Population: 7,364,570

Country: <u>Croatia</u>
Capital: Zagreb
Area(km²): 56,542
Population: 4,290,612

Country: <u>Czech Republic</u>
Capital: Prague
Area(km²): 78,866
Population: 10,722,870

Country: <u>Denmark</u>
Capital: Copenhagen
Area(km²): 43,094
Population: 5,813,290

Country: <u>Estonia</u>
Capital: Tallinn
Area(km²): 45,226
Population: 1,327,160

Country: <u>Finland</u>
Capital: Helsinki
Area(km²): 337,030
Population: 5,548,360

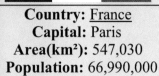

Country: <u>France</u>
Capital: Paris
Area(km²): 547,030
Population: 66,990,000

Country: <u>Germany</u>
Capital: Berlin
Area(km²): 357,021
Population: 83,900,470

Country: <u>Greece</u>
Capital: Athens
Area(km²): 131,940
Population:11,290,785

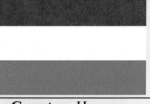

Country: <u>Hungary</u>
Capital: Budapest
Area(km²): 93,030
Population: 9,962,000

Country: <u>Iceland</u>
Capital: Reykjavik
Area(km²): 103,000
Population: 343,350

Country: <u>Ireland</u>
Capital: Dublin
Area(km²): 70,273
Population: 4,982,900

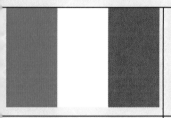

Country: <u>Italy</u>
Capital: Rome
Area(km²): 301,340
Population:
60,776,531

Country: <u>Latvia</u>
Capital: Riga
Area(km²): 64,589
Population: 1,900,000

Country:
<u>Liechtenstein</u>
Capital: Vaduz
Area(km²): 160
Population: 38,205

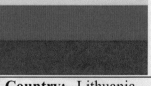

Country: <u>Lithuania</u>
Capital: Vilnius
Area(km²): 65,200
Population: 2,689,860

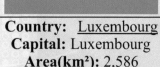

Country: <u>Luxembourg</u>
Capital: Luxembourg
Area(km²): 2,586
Population: 634,810

Country: <u>N.Macedonia</u>
Capital: Skopje
Area(km²): 25,333
Population: 2,083,310

Country: <u>Malta</u> **Capital:** Valletta **Area(km²):** 316 **Population:** 442,780	**Country:** <u>Moldova</u> **Capital:** Chisinau **Area(km²):** 33,846 **Population:** 4,024,100	**Country:** <u>Monaco</u> **Capital:** Monaco **Area(km²):** 2.02 **Population:** 39,444

Country: <u>Montenegro</u> **Capital:** Podgorica **Area(km²):** 14,026 **Population:** 632,796	**Country:** <u>Netherlands</u> **Capital:** Amsterdam **Area(km²):** 41,526 **Population:** 17,161,376	**Country:** <u>Norway</u> **Capital:** Oslo **Area(km²):** 385,186 **Population:** 5,400,000

Country: <u>Poland</u> **Capital:** Warsaw **Area(km²):** 312,685 **Population:**38,208,618	**Country:** <u>Portugal</u> **Capital:** Lisbon **Area(km²):** 92,082 **Population:** 10,541,840	**Country:** <u>Romania</u> **Capital:** Bucharest **Area(km²):** 237,500 **Population:** 19,130,000
Country: <u>Russia</u> **Capital:** Moscow **Area(km²):** 17,102,345 *(with territory in Asia)* **Population:** 143,400,000	**Country:** <u>San Marino</u> **Capital:** San Marino **Area(km²):** 61.00 **Population:** 33,981	**Country:** <u>Serbia</u> **Capital:** Belgrade **Area(km²):** 88,361 **Population:** 8,697,550

Country: <u>Slovakia</u>
Capital: Bratislava
Area(km²): 48,845
Population: 5,445,324

Country: <u>Slovenia</u>
Capital: Ljubljana
Area(km²): 20,253
Population: 2,080,400

Country: <u>Spain</u>
Capital: Madrid
Area(km²): 497,304
Population: 46,745,216

Country: <u>Sweden</u>
Capital: Stockholm
Area(km²): 449,964
Population:
10,161,000

Country: <u>Switzerland</u>
Capital: Bern
Area(km²): 41,290
Population: 8,715,500

Country: <u>Ukraine</u>
Capital: Kyiv
Area(km²): 603,628
Population: 43,466,900

Country: <u>United Kingdom</u>
Capital: London
Area(km²): 244,820
Population: 68,200,000

Country: <u>Vatican</u>
Capital: Vatican
Area(km²): 0.44
Population: 842

unrecognized states and states with limited recognition

Country: Kosovo
Capital: Pristina
(Recognized by
111 UN members)
Territory:
<u>Serbian</u>

Country:
Transnistria
Capital:
Tiraspol
Territory:
<u>Moldova</u>

Country: Luhansk
People's Republic
(LPR or LNR)
*illegally annexed in
2014*
Capital: Luhansk
Territory: <u>Ukraine</u>

Country: Donetsk
People's Republic
(DPR or DNR)
*illegally annexed in
2014*
Capital: Donetsk
Territory: <u>Ukraine</u>

United Kingdom

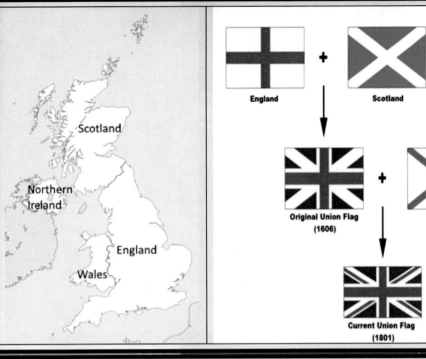

England + Scotland

Original Union Flag (1606) + Ireland

Current Union Flag (1801)

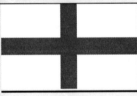

Country: England
Capital: London
Area (km²): 130,279
Population: 57,000,000

Country: Scotland
Capital: Edinburgh
Area (km²): 77,933
Population: 5,454,000

Country: Wales
Capital: Cardiff
Area (km²): 20,779
Population: 3,136,000

Country: Northern Ireland
Capital: Belfast
Area (km²): 14,130
Population: 1,980,000

AFRICA MAP

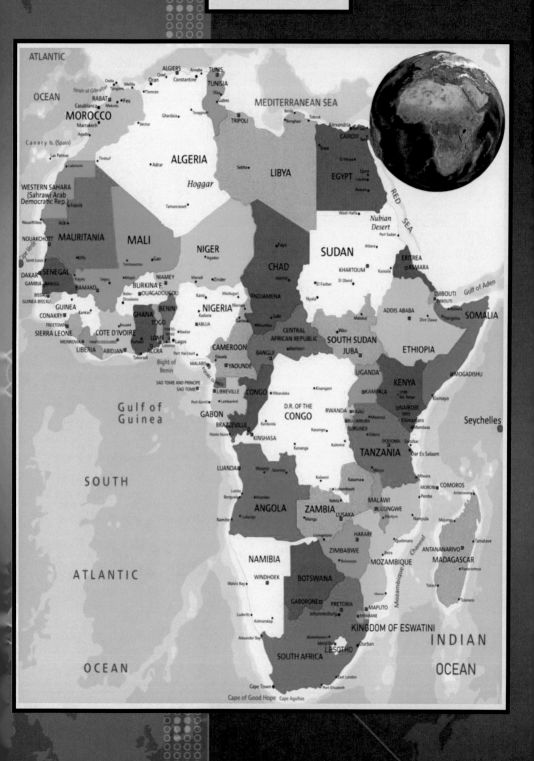

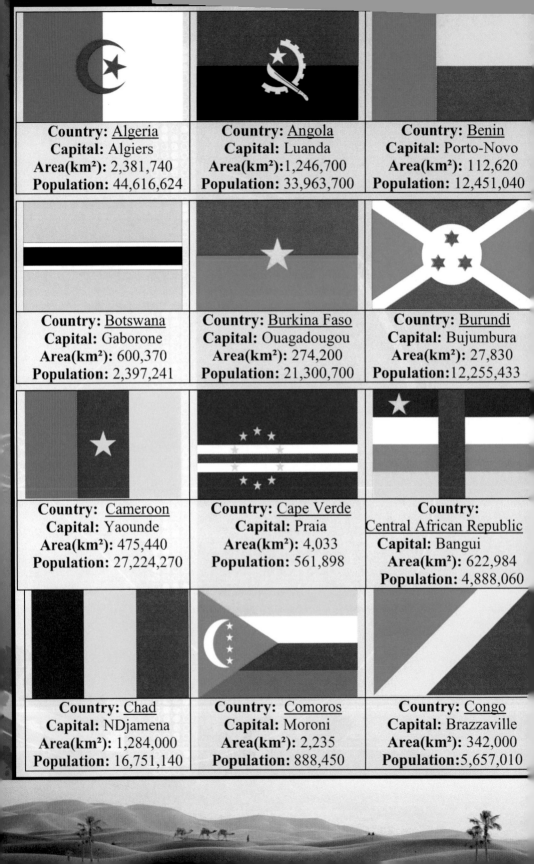

Country: <u>Algeria</u>
Capital: Algiers
Area(km²): 2,381,740
Population: 44,616,624

Country: <u>Angola</u>
Capital: Luanda
Area(km²): 1,246,700
Population: 33,963,700

Country: <u>Benin</u>
Capital: Porto-Novo
Area(km²): 112,620
Population: 12,451,040

Country: <u>Botswana</u>
Capital: Gaborone
Area(km²): 600,370
Population: 2,397,241

Country: <u>Burkina Faso</u>
Capital: Ouagadougou
Area(km²): 274,200
Population: 21,300,700

Country: <u>Burundi</u>
Capital: Bujumbura
Area(km²): 27,830
Population: 12,255,433

Country: <u>Cameroon</u>
Capital: Yaounde
Area(km²): 475,440
Population: 27,224,270

Country: <u>Cape Verde</u>
Capital: Praia
Area(km²): 4,033
Population: 561,898

Country:
<u>Central African Republic</u>
Capital: Bangui
Area(km²): 622,984
Population: 4,888,060

Country: <u>Chad</u>
Capital: NDjamena
Area(km²): 1,284,000
Population: 16,751,140

Country: <u>Comoros</u>
Capital: Moroni
Area(km²): 2,235
Population: 888,450

Country: <u>Congo</u>
Capital: Brazzaville
Area(km²): 342,000
Population: 5,657,010

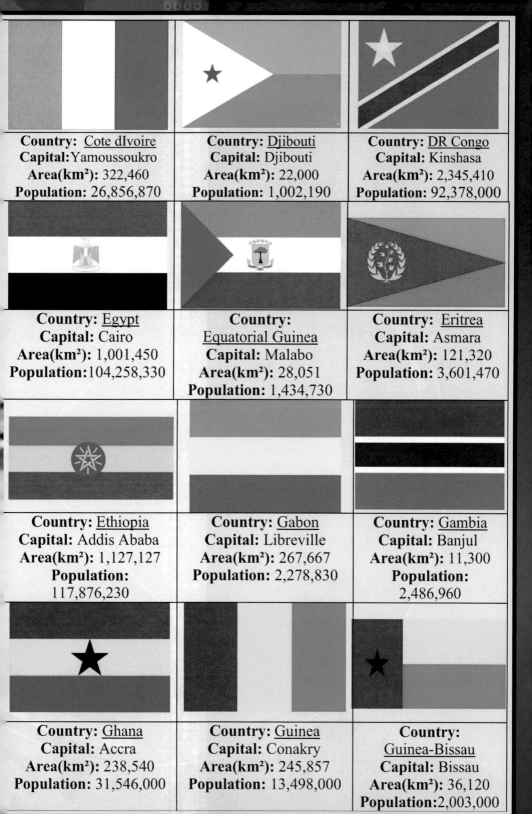

Country: Cote dIvoire
Capital: Yamoussoukro
Area(km²): 322,460
Population: 26,856,870

Country: Djibouti
Capital: Djibouti
Area(km²): 22,000
Population: 1,002,190

Country: DR Congo
Capital: Kinshasa
Area(km²): 2,345,410
Population: 92,378,000

Country: Egypt
Capital: Cairo
Area(km²): 1,001,450
Population: 104,258,330

Country:
Equatorial Guinea
Capital: Malabo
Area(km²): 28,051
Population: 1,434,730

Country: Eritrea
Capital: Asmara
Area(km²): 121,320
Population: 3,601,470

Country: Ethiopia
Capital: Addis Ababa
Area(km²): 1,127,127
Population:
117,876,230

Country: Gabon
Capital: Libreville
Area(km²): 267,667
Population: 2,278,830

Country: Gambia
Capital: Banjul
Area(km²): 11,300
Population:
2,486,960

Country: Ghana
Capital: Accra
Area(km²): 238,540
Population: 31,546,000

Country: Guinea
Capital: Conakry
Area(km²): 245,857
Population: 13,498,000

Country:
Guinea-Bissau
Capital: Bissau
Area(km²): 36,120
Population: 2,003,000

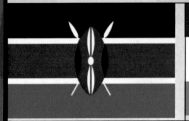

Country: <u>Kenya</u>	**Country:** <u>Lesotho</u>	**Country:** <u>Liberia</u>
Capital: Nairobi	**Capital:** Maseru	**Capital:** Monrovia
Area(km²): 582,650	**Area(km²):** 30,355	**Area(km²):** 111,370
Population: 55,000,000	**Population:** 2,216,850	**Population:** 5,140,000

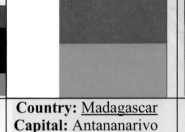

Country: <u>Libya</u>	**Country:** <u>Madagascar</u>	**Country:** <u>Malawi</u>
Capital: Tripoli	**Capital:** Antananarivo	**Capital:** Lilongwe
Area(km²): 1,759,540	**Area(km²):** 587,040	**Area(km²):** 118,480
Population: 6,999,000	**Population:** 28,428,000	**Population:** 19,648,000

Country: <u>Mali</u>	**Country:** <u>Mauritania</u>	**Country:** <u>Mauritius</u>
Capital: Bamako	**Capital:** Nouakchott	**Capital:** Port Louis
Area(km²): 1,240,000	**Area(km²):** 1,030,700	**Area(km²):** 2,040
Population: 20,856,000	**Population:** 4,740,000	**Population:** 1,280,294

Country: <u>Morocco</u>	**Country:** <u>Mozambique</u>	**Country:** <u>Namibia</u>
Capital: Rabat	**Capital:** Maputo	**Capital:** Windhoek
Area(km²): 446,550	**Area(km²):** 801,590	**Area(km²):** 825,418
Population: 37,219,000	**Population:** 32,164,000	**Population:** 2,588,000

Country: <u>Niger</u> **Capital:** Niamey **Area(km²):** 1,267,000 **Population:** 25,131,000	**Country:** <u>Nigeria</u> **Capital:** Abuja **Area(km²):** 923,768 **Population:** 213,400,000	**Country:** <u>Rwanda</u> **Capital:** Kigali **Area(km²):** 26,338 **Population:**13,277,000

Country: <u>Sao Tome and Principe</u> **Capital:** Sao Tome **Area(km²):** 1,001 **Population:** 222,000	**Country:** <u>Senegal</u> **Capital:** Dakar **Area(km²):** 196,190 **Population:** 17,197,000	**Country:** <u>Seychelles</u> **Capital:** Victoria **Area(km²):** 455 **Population:** 99,000

Country: <u>Sierra Leone</u> **Capital:** Freetown **Area(km²):** 71,740 **Population:** 8,090,000	**Country:** <u>Somalia</u> **Capital:** Mogadishu **Area(km²):** 637,657 **Population:** 16,360,000	**Country:** <u>South Africa</u> **Capital:** Pretoria **Area(km²):**1,219,912 **Population:** 59,829,000

Country: <u>South Sudan</u> **Capital:** Juba **Area(km²):** 619,745 **Population:**11,286,074	**Country:** <u>Sudan</u> **Capital:** Khartoum **Area(km²):** 1,886,068 **Population:** 44,910,000	**Country:** <u>Kingdom of Eswatini</u> **Capital:** Mbabane **Area(km²):** 17,363 **Population:** 1,169,000

Country: <u>Tanzania</u> **Capital:** Dodoma **Area(km²):** 948,087 **Population:**61,500,000	**Country:** <u>Togo</u> **Capital:** Lome **Area(km²):** 56,785 **Population:** 8,479,000	**Country:** <u>Tunisia</u> **Capital:** Tunis **Area(km²):** 163,610 **Population:**11,936,000

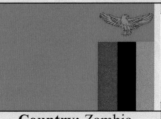

Country: <u>Uganda</u> **Capital:** Kampala **Area(km²):** 236,040 **Population:**47,124,000	**Country:** <u>Zambia</u> **Capital:** Lusaka **Area(km²):** 752,614 **Population:** 18,921,000	**Country:** <u>Zimbabwe</u> **Capital:** Harare **Area(km²):** 390,580 **Population:**15,093,000

unrecognized states and states with limited recognition

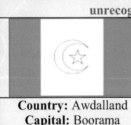
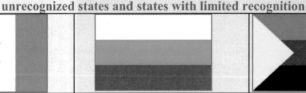
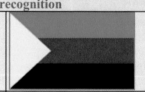

Country: Awdalland **Capital:** Boorama **Territory: Somalia**	**Country:** Azania **Capital:** Dhobley **Territory: Somalia**	**Country:** Azawad **Capital:** Timbuktu **Territory: Somalia**

Country: Galmudug **Capital:** Dhuusamareeb **Territory: Somalia**	**Country:**Himan and Heeb **Capital:** Adado **Territory: Somalia**	**Country:** Jubaland **Capital:** Kismayo **Territory: Somalia**

Country: Puntland **Capital:** Garowe **Territory: Somalia**	**Country:** Sahrawi Arab Democratic Republic (Recog. by 84 UN mem.) **Capital:** Laayoune **Ter: Morocco/Mauritania**	**Country:** Somaliland **Capital:** Hargeisa **Territory: Somalia**

Country: <u>Afghanistan</u> **Capital:** Kabul **Area(km²):** 647,500 **Population:** 39,836,000	**Country:** <u>Armenia</u> **Capital:** Yerevan **Area(km²):** 29,741 **Population:** 2,969,000	**Country:** <u>Azerbaijan</u> **Capital:** Baku **Area(km²):** 86,600 **Population:** 10,224,000

Country: <u>Bahrain</u> **Capital:** Manama **Area(km²):** 701 **Population:**1,749,000	**Country:** <u>Bangladesh</u> **Capital:** Dhaka **Area(km²):** 144,000 **Population:** 169,400,000	**Country:** <u>Bhutan</u> **Capital:** Thimphu **Area(km²):** 47,000 **Population:** 779,900

Country: <u>Brunei</u> **Capital:** Bandar Seri Begawan **Area(km²):** 5,770 **Population:** 442,000	**Country:** <u>Cambodia</u> **Capital:** Phnom Penh **Area(km²):** 181,040 **Population:** 16,947,000	**Country:** <u>China</u> **Capital:** Beijing **Area(km²):** 9,640,821 **Population:** 1,412,400,000
Country: <u>Cyprus</u> **Capital:** Nicosia **Area(km²):** 9,250 **Population:**1,216,000	**Country:** <u>East Timor</u> **Capital:** Dili **Area(km²):** 14,874 **Population:** 1,337,000	**Country:** <u>Georgia</u> (<u>Sakartvelo</u>) **Capital:** Tbilisi **Area(km²):** 69,700 **Population:** 3,984,000

Country: India **Capital:** New Delhi **Area(km²):** 3,287,590 **Population:** 1,425,700,000	**Country:** Indonesia **Capital:** Jakarta **Area(km²):** 1,904,556 **Population:** 273,800,000	**Country:** Iran **Capital:** Tehran **Area(km²):** 1,648,000 **Population:** 85,029,000
Country: Iraq **Capital:** Baghdad **Area(km²):** 437,072 **Population:** 40,882,000	**Country:** Israel **Capital:** Jerusalem **Area(km²):** 22,072 **Population:** 7,836,000	**Country:** Japan **Capital:** Tokyo **Area(km²):** 377,944 **Population:**127,300,000
		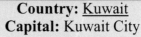
Country: Jordan **Capital:** Amman **Area(km²):**89,400 **Population:** 8,754,000	**Country:** Kazakhstan **Capital:** Astana **Area(km²):** 2,724,900 **Population:** 18,995,000	**Country:** Kuwait **Capital:** Kuwait City **Area(km²):** 17,820 **Population:** 4,316,000

Country: Kyrgyzstan **Capital:** Bishkek **Area(km²):** 198,500 **Population:** 6,599,000	**Country:** Laos **Capital:** Vientiane **Area(km²):** 236,800 **Population:** 7,349,000	**Country:** Lebanon **Capital:** Beirut **Area(km²):** 10,452 **Population:** 6,805,000

Country: <u>Malaysia</u> **Capital:** Kuala Lumpur **Area(km²):** 329,750 **Population:**32,777,000	**Country:** <u>Maldives</u> **Capital:** Male **Area(km²):** 300 **Population:** 543,800	**Country:** <u>Mongolia</u> **Capital:** Ulaanbaatar **Area(km²):** 1,564,116 **Population:** 3,330,800

Country: <u>Myanmar</u> **Capital:** Naypyidaw **Area(km²):** 678,500 **Population:**54,665,000	**Country:** <u>Nepal</u> **Capital:** Kathmandu **Area(km²):** 140,800 **Population:**29,517,000	**Country:** <u>North Korea</u> **Capital:** Pyongyang **Area(km²):** 120,540 **Population:**25,858,000

Country: <u>Oman</u> **Capital:** Muscat **Area(km²):** 309,500 **Population:**5,202,000	**Country:** <u>Pakistan</u> **Capital:** Islamabad **Area(km²):** 881,913 **Population:**231,400,000	**Country:** <u>Philippines</u> **Capital:** Manila **Area(km²):** 300,000 **Population:** 111,047,000

Country: <u>Qatar</u> **Capital:** Doha **Area(km²):** 11,437 **Population:**2,931,000	**Country:** <u>Saudi Arabia</u> **Capital:** Riyadh **Area(km²):** 2,218,000 **Population:**35,191,000	**Country:** <u>Singapore</u> **Capital:** Singapore **Area(km²):** 714 **Population:** 5,897,000

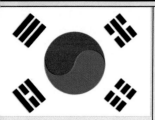

Country: South Korea
Capital: Seoul
Area(km²): 98,480
Population: 51,300,000

Country: Sri Lanka
Capital:
Sri Jayewardenepura Kotte
Area(km²): 65,610
Population: 21,476,000

Country:State of Palestine
Capital:East Jerusalem
(Ramallah)
Area(km²): 6,020
Population: 5,184,000

Country: Syria
Capital: Damascus
Area(km²): 185,180
Population:
18,092,000

Country: Tajikistan
Capital: Dushanbe
Area(km²): 143,100
Population: 9,750,000

Country: Thailand
Capital: Bangkok
Area(km²): 514,000
Population: 70,498,494

Country: Turkey
Capital: Ankara
Area(km²): 780,580
Population:
85,100,000

Country: Turkmenistan
Capital: Ashgabat
Area(km²): 491,200
Population: 6,118,000

Country:
United Arab Emirates
Capital: Abu Dhabi
Area(km²): 82,880
Population: 9,962,000

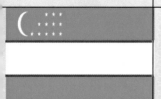

Country: Uzbekistan
Capital: Tashkent
Area(km²): 447,400
Population: 33,990,000

Country: Vietnam
Capital: Hanoi
Area(km²): 329,560
Population: 98,400,000

Country: Yemen
Capital: Sanaa
Area(km²): 527,970
Population: 30,500,000

unrecognized states and states with limited recognition

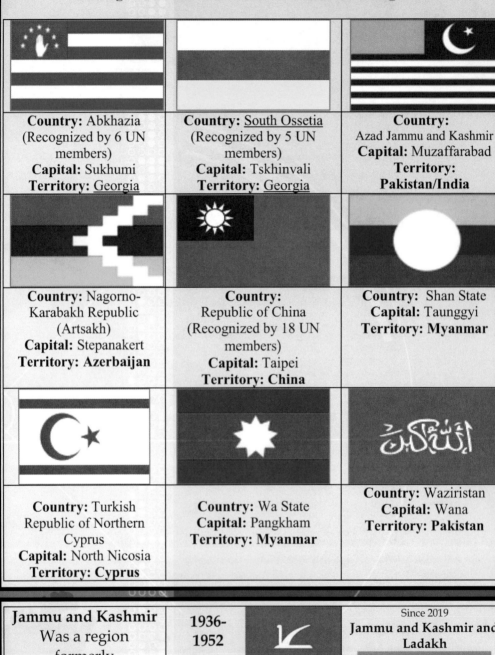

Country: Abkhazia (Recognized by 6 UN members)
Capital: Sukhumi
Territory: Georgia

Country: South Ossetia (Recognized by 5 UN members)
Capital: Tskhinvali
Territory: Georgia

Country: Azad Jammu and Kashmir
Capital: Muzaffarabad
Territory: Pakistan/India

Country: Nagorno-Karabakh Republic (Artsakh)
Capital: Stepanakert
Territory: Azerbaijan

Country: Republic of China (Recognized by 18 UN members)
Capital: Taipei
Territory: China

Country: Shan State
Capital: Taunggyi
Territory: Myanmar

Country: Turkish Republic of Northern Cyprus
Capital: North Nicosia
Territory: Cyprus

Country: Wa State
Capital: Pangkham
Territory: Myanmar

Country: Waziristan
Capital: Wana
Territory: Pakistan

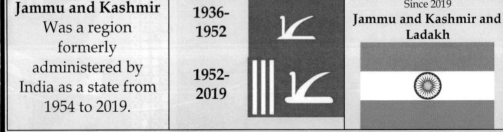

Jammu and Kashmir Was a region formerly administered by India as a state from 1954 to 2019.

1936-1952

1952-2019

Since 2019
Jammu and Kashmir and Ladakh

MAP OF AUSTRALIA AND OCEANIA

JAPAN

East China Sea

PHILIPPINES
Manila

Philippine Sea

Sulu Sea

Celebes Sea

MALAYSIA

Java Sea

Banda Sea

INDONESIA

Dili EAST TIMOR

Ceram Sea

Timor Sea

Arafura Sea

PALAU
Melekeok

GUAM

NORTHERN MARIANA ISLANDS

FEDERATED STATES OF MICRONESIA
Palikir

MARSHALL ISLANDS
Majuro

Tarawa

KIRIBATI

NAURU

SOLOMON ISLANDS
Honiara

Solomon Sea

Bismarck Sea

PAPUA NEW GUINEA

Port Moresby

Great Barrier Reef

Gulf of Carpentaria

AUSTRALIA

Canberra

Great Australian Bight

INDIAN OCEAN

VANUATU
Port Vila

NEW CALEDONIA

Coral Sea

TUVALU
Funafuti

FIJI
Suva

KIRIBATI

NORTH PACIFIC OCEAN

UNITED STATES

SAMOA
Apia

AMERICAN SAMOA

TONGA
Nukualofa

NIUE

COOK ISLANDS

FRENCH POLYNESIA

SOUTH PACIFIC OCEAN

PITCAIRN ISLANDS

NEW ZEALAND
Wellington

Tasman Sea

Country: <u>Australia</u>	**Country:**	**Country:** <u>Fiji</u>
Capital: Canberra	<u>Federated States of Micronesia</u>	**Capital:** Suva
Area(km²): 7,686,850	**Capital:** Palikir	**Area(km²):** 18,270
Population: 25,790,000	**Area(km²):** 702	**Population:** 903,000
	Population: 114,704	

Country: <u>Kiribati</u>	**Country:** <u>Marshall Islands</u>	**Country:** <u>Nauru</u>
Capital: Tarawa Atoll	**Capital:** Majuro	**Capital:** [no capital]
Area(km²): 717	**Area(km²):** 181	**Area(km²):** 21.30
Population: 121,500	**Population:** 59,600	**Population:** 10,900

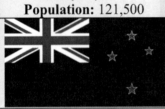

Country: <u>New Zealand</u>	**Country:** <u>Palau</u>	**Country:**
Capital: Wellington	**Capital:** Ngerulmud	<u>Papua New Guinea</u>
Area(km²): 268,680	**Area(km²):** 458	**Capital:** Port Moresby
Population: 4,859,000	**Population:** 20,609	**Area(km²):** 463,840
		Population: 9,170,000

Country: <u>Samoa</u>	**Country** <u>Solomon Islands</u>	**Country:** <u>Tonga</u>
Capital: Apia	**Capital:** Honiara	**Capital:** Nukualofa
Area(km²): 2,860	**Area(km²):** 28,450	**Area(km²):** 748
Population: 200,200	**Population:** 704,000	**Population:** 106,891

Country: <u>Tuvalu</u>	**Country:** <u>Vanuatu</u>
Capital: Funafuti	**Capital:** Port-Vila
Area(km²): 26.00	**Area(km²):** 12,200
Population: 12,000	**Population:** 314,600

TRANSCONTINENTAL COUNTRIES

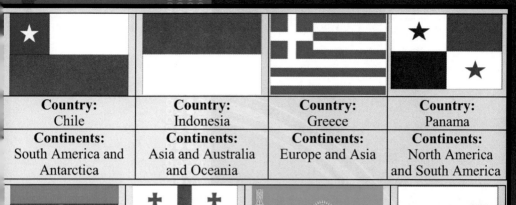

Country: Chile	Country: Indonesia	Country: Greece	Country: Panama
Continents: South America and Antarctica	Continents: Asia and Australia and Oceania	Continents: Europe and Asia	Continents: North America and South America

Country: Azerbaijan	Country: Georgia	Country: Kazakhstan	Country: Russia
Continents: Asia and Europe	Continents: Asia and Europe	Continents: Asia and Europe	Continents: Asia and Europe

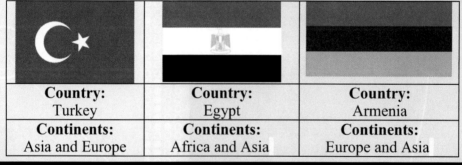

Country: Turkey	Country: Egypt	Country: Armenia
Continents: Asia and Europe	Continents: Africa and Asia	Continents: Europe and Asia

STATES OF THE UNITED STATES OF AMERICA

Name:	Capital (Largest):	Total area mi² (km²):	Population:	Became a State
Alabama	Montgomery (Birmingham)	52,420 (135,767)	4,874,747	December 14, 1819
Alaska	Juneau (Anchorage)	665,384 (1,723,337)	739,795	January 3, 1959
Arizona	Phoenix	113,990 (295,234)	7,016,270	February 14, 1912
Arkansas	Little Rock	53,179 (137,732)	3,004,279	June 15, 1836
California	Sacramento (Los Angeles)	163,695 (423,967)	39,536,653	September 9, 1850
Colorado	Denver	104,094 (269,601)	5,607,154	August 1, 1876
Connecticut	Hartford (Bridgeport)	5,543 (14,357)	3,588,184	January 9, 1788

Name:	Capital (Largest):	Total area mi² (km²):	Population:	Became a State
Delaware	Dover (Wilmington)	2,489 (6,446)	961,939	December 7, 1787
Florida	Tallahassee (Jacksonville)	65,758 (170,312)	20,984,400	March 3, 1845
Georgia	Atlanta	59,425 (153,910)	10,429,379	January 2, 1788
Hawaii	Honolulu	10,932 (28,313)	1,427,538	August 21, 1959
Idaho	Boise	83,569 (216,443)	1,716,943	July 3, 1890
Illinois	Springfield (Chicago)	57,914 (149,995)	12,802,023	December 3, 1818
Indiana	Indianapolis	36,420 (94,326)	6,666,818	December 11, 1816
Iowa	Des Moines	56,273 (145,746)	3,145,711	December 28, 1846

Name:	Capital (Largest):	Total area mi² (km²):	Population:	Became a State
Kansas	Topeka (Wichita)	82,278 (213,100)	2,913,123	January 29, 1861
Kentucky	Frankfort (Louisville)	40,408 (104,656)	4,454,189	June 1, 1792
Louisiana	Baton Rouge (New Orleans)	52,378 (135,659)	4,684,333	April 30, 1812
Maine	Augusta (Portland)	35,380 (91,633)	1,335,907	March 15, 1820
Maryland	Annapolis (Baltimore)	12,406 (32,131)	6,052,177	April 28, 1788
Massachusetts	Boston	10,554 (27,336)	6,859,819	February 6, 1788
Michigan	Lansing (Detroit)	96,714 (250,487)	9,962,311	January 26, 1837
Minnesota	St. Paul (Minneapolis)	86,936 (225,163)	5,576,606	May 11, 1858

Name:	Capital (Largest):	Total area mi² (km²):	Population:	Became a State
Mississippi	Jackson	48,432 (125,438)	2,984,100	December 10, 1817
Missouri	Jefferson City (Kansas City)	69,707 (180,540)	6,113,532	August 10, 1821
Montana	Helena (Billings)	147,040 (380,831)	1,050,493	November 8, 1889
Nebraska	Lincoln (Omaha)	77,348 (200,330)	1,920,076	March 1, 1867
Nevada	Carson City (Las Vegas)	110,572 (286,380)	2,998,039	October 31, 1864
New Hampshire	Concord (Manchester)	9,349 (24,214)	1,342,795	June 21, 1788
New Jersey	Trenton (Newark)	8,723 (22,591)	9,005,644	December 18, 1787
New Mexico	Santa Fe (Albuquerque)	121,590 (314,917)	2,088,070	January 6, 1912

Name:	Capital (Largest):	Total area mi² (km²):	Population:	Became a State
New York	Albany (New York City)	54,555 (141,297)	19,849,399	July 26, 1788
North Carolina	Raleigh (Charlotte)	53,819 (139,391)	10,273,419	November 21, 1789
North Dakota	Bismarck (Fargo)	70,698 (183,108)	755,393	November 2, 1889
Ohio	Columbus	44,826 (116,098)	11,658,609	March 1, 1803
Oklahoma	Oklahoma City	69,899 (181,037)	3,930,864	November 16, 1907
Oregon	Salem (Portland)	98,379 (254,799)	4,142,776	February 14, 1859
Pennsylvania	Harrisburg (Philadelphia)	46,054 (119,280)	12,805,537	December 12, 1787
Rhode Island	Providence	1,545 (4,001)	1,059,639	May 19, 1790

Name:	Capital (Largest):	Total area mi² (km²):	Population:	Became a State
South Carolina	Columbia (Charleston)	32,020 (82,933)	5,024,369	May 23, 1788
South Dakota	Pierre (Sioux Falls)	77,116 (199,729)	869,666	November 2, 1889
Tennessee	Nashville	42,144 (109,153)	6,715,984	June 1, 1796
Texas	Austin (Houston)	268,596 (695,662)	28,304,596	December 29, 1845
Utah	Salt Lake City	84,897 (219,882)	3,101,833	January 4, 1896
Vermont	Montpelier (Burlington)	9,616 (24,906)	623,657	March 4, 1791
Virginia	Richmond (Virginia Beach)	42,775 (110,787)	8,470,020	June 25, 1788
Washington	Olympia (Seattle)	71,298 (184,661)	7,405,743	November 11, 1889

Name:	Capital (Largest):	Total area mi² (km²):	Population:	Became a State
West Virginia	Charleston	24,230 (62,756)	1,815,857	June 20, 1863
Wisconsin	Madison (Milwaukee)	65,496 (169,635)	5,795,483	May 29, 1848
Wyoming	Cheyenne	97,813 (253,335)	579,315	July 10, 1890

Territories

Name: American Samoa
Capital: Pago Pago
Area mi² (km²): 581 (1,505)
Population: 57,400

Name: Guam
Capital: Hagåtña
Area mi² (km²): 571 (1,478)
Population: 161,700

Name: Northern Mariana Islands
Capital: Saipan
Area mi² (km²): 1,976 (5,117)
Population: 52,300

Name: Puerto Rico
Capital: San Juan
Area mi² (km²): 5,325 (13,791)
Population: 3,337,177

Name: U.S. Virgin Islands
Capital: Charlotte Amalie
Area mi² (km²): 733 (1,898)
Population: 103,700

Federal district

District of Columbia	**Total Area mi² (km²):** 68 (176) **Population:** 693,972